Jungle Animals

PARROTS

By Rob Ryndak

Gareth Stevens
PUBLISHING

Please visit our website, www.garethstevens.com. For a free color catalog of all our high-quality books, call toll free 1-800-542-2595 or fax 1-877-542-2596.

Library of Congress Cataloging-in-Publication Data

Ryndak, Rob.
Parrots / by Rob Ryndak.
p. cm. — (Jungle animals)
Includes index.
ISBN 978-1-4824-1757-9 (pbk.)
ISBN 978-1-4824-1758-6 (6-pack)
ISBN 978-1-4824-1756-2 (library binding)
1. Parrots — Juvenile literature. I. Title.
QL696.P7 R96 2015
598.7—d23

First Edition

Published in 2015 by
Gareth Stevens Publishing
111 East 14th Street, Suite 349
New York, NY 10003

Editor: Ryan Nagelhout
Designer: Katelyn E. Reynolds

Photo credits: Cover, pp. 1, 24 (parrot) Mircea BEZERGHEANU/Shutterstock.com; p. 5 Lucky Business/Shutterstock.com; p. 7 altrendo nature/Getty Images; p. 9 Stanislav Komogorov/Shutterstock.com; p. 11 Herbert Eisengruber/Shutterstock.com; pp. 13, 24 (nuts) AJE/Shutterstock.com; p. 15 NICOLAS ASFOURI/AFP/Getty Images; p. 17 Alta Oosthuizen/Shutterstock.com; p. 19 Cbenjasuwan/Shutterstock.com; p. 21 Meaning/Shutterstock.com; p. 23 Jill Lang/Shutterstock.com.

Printed in the United States of America

CPSIA compliance information: Batch #CW15GS: For further information contact Gareth Stevens, New York, New York at 1-800-542-2595.

Contents

Parrots are very bright birds.

There are more than 350 kinds.

They are many colors.

Parrots love to eat fruit.

They also like nuts.

They live a long time.
Many live
up to 80 years!

They make many kinds of sounds.

They love to sing.

Parrots can even talk! They can say words they hear.

Many people keep them as pets.

Words to Know

nut

parrot

Index